BECOME A CONSULTANT

SECRETS FROM A PROFESSIONAL TO CREATE YOUR PERFECT LIFE

L D FORESTER

Printed in the United States of America

First Edition – February 2018

Paperback
978-0-9911007-7-4
0-9911007-7-8

LD Media and Twin Creek Publishing
Copyright © 2018

DEDICATION

To my dad, who taught me
about to taking risks
and enjoying life.

BECOME A CONSULTANT

CONTENTS

ABOUT THE AUTHOR

After working 80-100 hours per week next to consultants who were getting paid for each hour they worked, L D Forester left a corporate career about 2 decades ago, opting to become a fulltime consultant.

LD's off consultancy periods are filled with extraordinary experiences volunteering and exploring the planet, able to do so because of the decision to go into consultancy.

"I've never felt more alive as I strive to break free of the conventional means in which most make their living. I wish you all the success in your new way of living as you breathe the sweet fragrance of the deliciousness of life." L D Forester

INTRODUCTION

I was inspired to write this book while on a consulting assignment.

It's when we dare to move in new and different directions that we find our strengths, talents, inspiration and purpose.

There was a period in my life when I worked as a fulltime employee in the corporate world, moving toward consultancy about 20 years ago. With so many years working in consultancy, it was pointed out to me that my vast experience to help others would be wasted if not shared.

This book explains techniques to secure ideal consulting assignments in this digital age, as it shows you ways to maximize your reach, where networking takes care of itself. It describes ways to search and procure assignments with no out-of-pocket costs and includes tricks, so your résumé appears on the first page of job engine searches by potential clients with less than a 10-minute effort per day.

It describes a different way of looking at employment, and living based on enjoyment and enrichment as you take back control of your life.

No matter what your goals are for consulting in this new era, the information in these pages provides you with new avenues of enjoying your life while earning.

1
CREATING YOUR LIFE AS A CONSULTANT

Depending on the way you approach employment and consultancy, you'll have more freedom to experience a more enriched self-created life, filled with adventure and expansion. You just decide to live like a consultant and determine how to spend your time-off prior to canvasing for your next consulting assignment when you're ready to jump back into the job market. That's right you heard me, when *you* are ready to work again.

You are taking back control of your life.

Whether male or female, if you're guided to this book, perhaps it's time to take that leap of faith into consultancy.

For some of you who've been working for the same firm forever, or those who are tied to a same location for decades, there are still options for you in consultancy.

And I know it can be a bit frightening, so perhaps the below will help you move forward:

Making a big life change can be scary. You know what's even more frightening? Regret

2

A New Way of Looking at Employment

Defining Yourself by Your Corporate Status

I've met tons of people that define themselves by their corporate status. Rising to the level of vice president, managing many initiatives in technology, I certainly wore my prior corporate title as a badge for all to see, mostly to impress myself as well as the people that I met.

As a consultant, picking my assignments and no longer tied to one corporation, I only have compassion for those people who puff themselves up by their title, as I think to myself, I used to be one of you poor souls.

I interact with a ton of people who tell me how they are feeling and how they view themselves. Overall, people are just not happy. They lack that elated feeling each day, continually living with blinders on, oblivious to a more wonderful life that's right in front of them. For most that I speak with they live entangled in the rat race, striving to get to the top of the corporate ladder, gaining the biggest title, home, car and things, thinking that once they achieve all the goals they set out for themselves, they'll experience joy.

I'm not saying that there's anything wrong with money and nice things. I love money and nice things, but neither has value when it comes to inner joy. It's knowing this that keeps me in consultancy to fund my lifestyle of living for enjoyment.

If you can relate to any of the above, then maybe it's time to change the way you look at life and employment, realizing what's you value most in life. For me it's the times shared with those I love, the joy I experience when traveling and that great feeling that I get inside when I help someone. Okay, so maybe I'm getting a little too philosophical for this book, so let's get back to consulting.

It was 1996 when I was working in Washington, DC, as a manager for an application development team. I was young back then, already moving up the rungs of the corporate ladder, as evidenced by the large windowed corner office outfitted with my own couch and conference table. I certainly thought I'd made it.

I toiled side-by-side with consultants from pre-dawn to midnight as we worked toward the satisfaction of deadlines. I commented that I had worked about 387 hours that month. I said it proudly as if I had won some sort of prize. It was the consultant's reply that would change my perception forever.

*"You do realize that I **got paid** for every hour that I worked. You on the other hand accepted a 60% decrease in your pay to be here working alongside me."*

It took a few moments for me to do the math in my head, then it dawned on me. If the average work month is 160 hours (40 hours a week for 4 weeks), then he was right, I worked an extra 227 hours that month for free. Sure, I had this big office and a great title, but that and a few bonus dollars and a promise of a pension decades down the road was not enough to make up the difference here.

It was then that I started to talk to him about becoming a consultant.

As I look back on that faithful night, I realized that what he shared with me was eye opening.

BREAKING THE MYTH

This is where I'm going to say something that's a complete contradiction to what most of us were taught from the time when we understood that life was not just playing with toys. It was certainly drilled into me throughout my lifetime by my mother who preached about the value of a good position within a firm, then after 35 or 40 years, a solid retirement fund. Well, that's what she always said to my dad who gave up the corporate lifestyle in pursuit of his dream of being an entrepreneur.

Today I think that working in a single firm your entire career does not benefit you.

It's no longer the 70's, 80's or 90's, when not staying in the same position for at least 5 years destroys careers.

As a matter of fact, moving after 2 to 3 years in may be more expansive to your skillset than if you stayed in the same company.

And you know why, right?

It's because innovation and technology in the last decade has changed faster than any one single firm can keep up with it, so moving to firms utilizing the newest technologies and methodologies will be more beneficial to your skillset, making you more marketable while putting more money in your pocket.

This theory holds true whether you're a fulltime employee in a firm or decide to become a consultant.

Either way you want to continue to expand and grow. In this instance, complacency is not your friend. While working as a full-time employee in firms, the 2-year mark in an existing position always had me seeking out new challenges in different areas within the company.

Doing this afforded me the opportunity of trying something new while getting paid for the new experience. What a win-win for me. And I was such a diligent worker that management was always pleased with my work product. Being a fast learner, I was able to jump into new areas and quickly assimilate. It was something that allowed me to easily transition from fulltime employment to consultancy.

A NEW ERA DEFINES EMPLOYMENT

If you haven't figured it out by now, I don't have a very traditional approach to life or employment. Perhaps that's not a bad thing and it certainly stems from my upbringing, my desire to live my purpose, and create the life I want. What I share with you in the coming sections of this book is the mindset for taking that leap into the unknown and landing on your feet in the job market, giving you the options of working from the comfort of your home, or in a new city with each new assignment, or perhaps a new country.

To determine if consultancy is something you should consider, ask yourself these questions.

Are you a young professional who has at least 2-5 years of experience looking to drastically increase your income?

Are you a seasoned professional wanting to beef up your retirement savings your last few years of employment?

Are you a recent retiree with decades of experience looking to dabble in consultancy part of the year?

Are you not tied to a single place and looking to venture out into the world?

Are you looking to spend time abroad and explore?

Does the thought of potentially working in your pajamas sound appealing?

If the answer to any of these questions is yes, then perhaps there is a consultancy assignment made just for you.

In the last 2 decades, I've met more people like me, who work a 6 to 24-month assignment, then take 6 to 24 months off to enjoy their life. Some are young professionals, others empty nesters or recently single with no ties, looking for a new start and others are couples, who travel to new locations in their home country or abroad as they look for ways to enrich their family's cultural experiences.

When I think about consulting as I write this chapter, I'm reminded of a movie with a famous actor whose first name is George, who lived his life on the road. That does not necessarily have to be the case.

I did spend the first 15 years of my career traveling as a fulltime employee, but with consultancy, there's a vast amount of opportunity. It includes assignments in your area, others where you travel to the job site several days a week, or as little to one week per month, and others still, where working remote is an option. It all depends on how in demand your skillset is and what you negotiate.

There have been times in my life where I was living very lean and have taken onsite opportunities, although these days working remote with some travel to the client site is my ideal situation.

I remember a short assignment I had where I was brought in to analyze a set of systems for a large pharmaceutical firm in Texas. I was onsite for the entire 16 weeks of the assignment detailing current processes and work flows.

When the firm called me back to manage a long-term project at their east coast location, I told them that I would consider it if I could work onsite for the first 12 weeks, then remote for the remainder of the contract with a 1 week per month onsite commitment. They agreed.

As in anything in life, if you prove that you stand out in the crowd and know how to negotiate, you make your own opportunities.

3

WHAT JOBS ARE AVAILABLE TO CONSULTANCY

When I first started in consultancy, I was not aware of many of the opportunities that are afforded to this line of work, thinking it was mainly business management and technology that bred the most consultants.

Theoretically, any position can be farmed out to a consultant with the right skillset. Here are a few that I'm aware of, but I'm sure that there are many more.

- Accountants
- Auditors
- Business Analysts
- Compliance Experts
- Consultants traveling to countries in conflict or rebuild countries infrastructure after conflict
- Educators and Trainers
- Remote and traveling Medical Coders

- On-loan staff for hospitals when there's a conflict with existing workers
- Program Managers
- Project Managers
- Quality Assurance Experts and Testing Staff
- Quality Medical Reviewers
- Resume Writers
- Software Developers
- System Analysts
- System Architects
- Technical Writers
- Traveling Doctors and Nurses

I remember when my primary physician was pregnant. As the time of her delivery neared, she hired a consulting MD to come in and take her place. This afforded her the opportunity to provide coverage for her existing patients and well as keep a positive cash flow and employment for her existing staff, by not closing the office. I spoke to the consulting physician who explained to me that she only takes assignments 3 times a year. Her criteria included a duration of 10 to 12 weeks, for a total of 30 to 36 weeks annually. When I asked her what she does in her downtime, she explained that she had a small place in the French countryside where she goes when her current assignments end. She further detailed that her work is obtained through agents based on the schedule she supplies to them regarding her availability.

In my family, consultancy is becoming a trend, with my sister as a certified remote medical coder. She gained a few years of experience working for a health organization before becoming a consultant. Now she makes her own hours, has doubled her pay rate and can live pretty much anywhere without restrictions.

I say this, but know that some US companies require their remote workforce to live within the United States. For every rule though, there is an exception. I knew a consultant named Brent, back in the earlier part of the millennium who worked remotely 6 months of the year from an apartment he rented in Spain. This was part of his negotiation with the firm after he worked with them for a year. He was so good, they didn't want to lose him, so agreed to his terms. I've never worked a remote US assignment while living abroad, but would consider doing so if the opportunity presented itself.

I want to point out that if you're working remotely, living in an area that's in a different time zone than the client, that you'll need to be flexible to work the same core hours as the members located in the central team location. This is something that I mention when speaking to clients about remote assignments to ensure that they know that I am willing and able to be on calls, before 7 am or late into the evening, if required.

TEMP HELP VERSUS CONSULTANCY

I want to clarify that when I speak about consultancy that I'm not referring to seasonal workers. Although these jobs are valuable, they're categorized as temp jobs, not consultancy. The pay rates of temp jobs are usually in-line with the same pay rates received by the firm's fulltime staff, whereas consultants typically receive higher rates than the fulltime employees working in a company.

4
THE DECISION TO BECOME A CONSULTANT

It's been such a long time since I followed the more traditional employment path that it almost seems as if it was another lifetime. I'm not knocking that traditional path, for many still follow it today, some of whom are my friends and family. It just no longer serves me or works as part of my way of living.

For me, it's about working to live, not living to work. I live a less than traditional life, not tied to many material possessions. Toward that end, my view of employment has changed so much over past decades as I enjoy taking time off in between consulting assignments to write, speak and volunteer as I explore this wonderful planet.

Writing and lecturing is my dream and my passion. It is this passion that has been realized because I made the decision to abandon the traditional mindset of the corporate structure to become a consultant.

HAVING SKILLS CORPORATIONS ARE SEEKING

Consultants make top dollar because they offer a skillset and expertise that's in demand.

Often when I'm in a new place, meeting people in the area, they ask what I do for a living. When I tell them that I'm a consultant, working when I want, for whom I choose, at a rate I negotiate and that I take time to travel between assignments, they most often say, *"Wow, how can I get a job like that?"*

If you look at the sentence at the top of this section, it's clear that you <u>must</u> have a few years of experience under your belt as well as marketable skills and in some cases certifications to be a consultant.

Graduating college or technical school does not constitute an entitlement to jump into consultancy and make the big bucks. I continually chuckle when I meet a young kid who is getting ready to graduate college, thinking that he's going to start at a firm and make over $100,000 his first year out of the gate. You must be realistic. So, let me say this again: You need real world experience to be marketable in consultancy.

That said, I have noticed that the time to gain the experience you need has been drastically reduced from when I first started in this business. Having a dozen years of experience in a line of business or technology is no longer the rule. I've seen companies hiring junior consultants with as little as 2 to3 years of experience within a skillset or market niche. The rate may be lower than a senior consultant, but most often the hourly pay is leaps and bounds above what these same people were earning working directly for a firm.

So, kids, you do have to pay your dues, but 2-3 years is not forever! I promise, that the older you get, the faster time will fly by.

5
SEARCHING OUT THE IDEAL ASSIGNMENT

So, you've decided to move into consultancy. Or perhaps you're already a consultant and want to know some tips on seeking out your next assignment.

This is where the pavement meets the road, for a consultancy is only good when you are adding value to a company, while also adding to, or increasing your skillset.

Let me clarify a few things for you regarding what I mean by the above.

In consultancy, there must be something that the company is gaining from the arrangement; your expertise. There is also something that you need to gain as well, outside of a hefty paycheck at the end of every week. Yes, the paycheck is nice, but you also receive a paycheck as a fulltime employee. Part of what you seek in every assignment is to come away with a new marketable skill, or more experience in an existing competency that you can use for procuring your next assignment.

Another thing to consider is what duration of assignment you want to work. Longer is not always better. It all depends on your circumstances, financial or otherwise. For example, I took a 6-month remote assignment from fall to spring because I planned a summer long Europe vacation. This is the kind of flexibility that consultancy provides, if you know how to market and negotiate.

FACTORS TO CONSIDER

When your inbox is full of requests for your talent, in addition to determining if you meet the job description's skill requirements, you want to think about how accepting the assignment will benefit you in the long run, as well as fully understand the duration and the rate you will be paid.

Research
Ideally you want to do your homework prior to the submission of your qualifications to potential clients. That's not always the case when dealing with agencies, since they usually only have a

limited amount of information when receiving a job request. Prior to submission, you can find out the location, duration, rate and high-level description. Using the Internet, you can also perform your research about the client company. Any questions that remain can be obtained during the initial phone screen. It's here that you're given the opportunity to ask questions after the client explains the assignment's roles and responsibilities. This is discussed in more detail in the Interviewing chapter of this book.

Remember how I said that there must be something in it for you, the consultant to consider the assignment? Today I ask a few qualifying questions before I hit the delete key. Here are factors I use when considering onsite assignments, like:

- My monetary circumstances
- Rate and paid expense policy
- Location: Weather/Time of Year
- Duration
- Additions to my skillset

Monetary Circumstances

If I have correctly planned, I will never be in a situation where I am down to my last few dollars. But there are times where I have found myself in that situation due to unforeseen changes in the economic climate. A perfect example was when I had finished a consulting assignment and went on a 4-month vacation. I was locked in, or so I thought to a 4-year government contract that would begin in late September 2001.

Then 9/11 happened, and all bets were off, as I watched my contract start date get pushed, then cancelled. The entire country was unsettled and consulting work was hard to come by.

Although this has been the exception to the rule, I've worked onsite in an out of state location because of monetary lean times.

Rate and Paid Expense Policy

I use a base rate for a local onsite assignment that is within a 20-minute drive of my home. I alter that rate up or down depending on whether the contract is remote. requires me to travel and has expenses paid.

The Rates section in this book provides information to help you determine your base rate and calculate the cost of living for out of state assignments.

Location: Weather/Time of Year

Maybe I'm just spoiled, but when an agent sends me a request to work in Minneapolis or Chicago over the winter, or Phoenix or Houston in the summer, I immediately shutter. I prefer to live an incredible life, which includes incredible weather.

I do not, however, automatically dismiss the location if there is something beneficial to gain from the arrangement, like a new skill.

Duration

Along with weather, I consider the duration of an assignment based on location, if that may bring me into a new season. I may not want to work more than a 6-month assignment if it's in one of the locations I mention above unless I can work remotely part of the time when the weather is not desirable. I also look at shorter duration assignments paying me more than long term ones.

If it's a 3-month local assignment, and my base rate is $50, I may add a 50% markup to $75 per hour, since very short assignments do not help your resume and I may have to canvas for my next assignment again quickly based on my monetary health.

Additions to My Skillset

One question I ask myself when taking on a new assignment, whether it is remote, close to home or out of state, is if there is some addition I will gain to my skillset or some other factors that will benefit me down the road.

For example, there was a recent assignment where they wanted me in Hartford and Boston 4 days per week from November through the end of the following summer. Although I am not a fan of snow, the new skill gained, the great rate, the ability to work remote one day per week, full expense reimbursement, 80% paid health insurance as well as the airline and hotel elite status and points gained, made this an opportunity that I could not pass up.

After the assignment, the miles and points gained in that prior 10-month period, resulted in 3 months of free vacation travel, outside of food costs.

6

RATES: HOW MUCH CAN I EXPECT TO MAKE

As I put my fingers to keyboard to write this chapter, I'm reminded of the time when I made more money than I had time to spend. It was late 1999 as companies were offering very high hourly rates as the Y2K scare was in full swing. I worked tirelessly 80+hour weeks managing technology projects as the dreaded January 1, 2000 deadline approached.

When all was said and done, Y2K was not the big deal so many analysts made it out to be. The world did not stop in its tracks and business went on as usual.

The assignment lasted toward the middle of 2000 as we ensured all system issues were resolved. Now complete, I took a long deserved and overdue break to recharge and spend some of the money that I had accumulated in my checking account, more than enough for my dream car, a new Porsche 911 Cabriolet.

The above story explains the kind of money that a consultant can make if circumstances are just right.

Supply and demand will directly impact the rate that you can charge your clients. In the above situation, companies were panicking. And in a time of panic, the available pool of people in consultancy was very small. As with all times when supply is low and demand high, the price for talented consultants went way up, since consultants are a commodity.

I do finish my Porsche story in the chapter labeled, *How to Live Like a Consultant*.

DIFFERENT TYPES OF RATES

Below are the different types of hourly rates:

- W2
- 1099
- C2C (Corp to Corp)

Each one of the above options has its pros and cons as well as tax consequences, outlined in a later chapter in this book.

DETERMINING YOUR BASE RATE

The rule of thumb for base consulting rates is to take your current annual income and multiple it by 50% for a local assignment. Take the adjusted annual income and divide it by 2000 to get your base W2 rate.

I also suggest looking on career sites and filtering for contracts in your desired area of expertise to see what companies are currently paying for your skillset.

PLUS EXPENSES VS INCLUSIVE RATE

Companies and agencies will provide information on whether the rate is inclusive or plus expenses. Expenses include but are not limited to weekly or monthly travel, food lodging and local transportation.

An inclusive rate is the per hour rate that you will receive regardless of the expenses required for being onsite.

It may seem obvious to you the difference between an inclusive and plus expenses rate, but know that these are things to consider when accepting an assignment.

Using an example of $75 an hour to work onsite close to my house, I would accept $60 an hour to work 100% from home, the $15 per hour decrease for the increased convenience of being able to work in my pajamas, cook and do laundry and other small chores during the workday. If the client is paying for travel and lodging expenses and I must be onsite in another state, then perhaps $90 an hour would be acceptable to me to take this travel assignment, the extra $15 per hour to make up for the fact that I am not enjoying my home state. I may consider an inclusive contract in Chicago if the rate was $125 an hour to cover all, the extra $50 per hour covering my inconvenience and travel expenses.

When working on an assignment that is not 100% remote and does not include paid expenses, it must, and I can't stress this enough, must be profitable for you to consider consulting at this location, considering all factors including convenience. If the client does not pay expenses, I need an idea of how much it will cost me to live in the client location while on assignment.

I've created a Consulting Rate Estimator to weigh the differences of the cost of living for the locations I'm considering based on the government GSA Per Diem Rates to calculate my break-even hourly rate. I use it to adjust my rate accordingly.

Profitability is determined by calculating the cost of living for out of state assignments for the break-even rate using standard daily lodging rates.

You'll find the current year's Consulting Rate Estimator on LDForester.com under the Tools menu.

This chart is crucial to me when I'm asked to provide an all-inclusive rate to an agent prior to submission. For those of you are not familiar with this term, an all-inclusive hourly rate is the hourly rate you will accept for the assignment that includes your costs for travel, food and lodging. You will pay tax on the entire rate versus expense reimbursement, but there are pros to an all-inclusive rate that we will discuss in a later section of this book.

After I look at my rate chart, I find the cost of a hotel in the general area and accordingly adjust my rate to calculate my all-inclusive rate. My rule of thumb in more expensive cities is that my first hour working should at least cover my nightly lodging expense. In less expensive cities, that lodging rate should equate to 50% to 75%. A less senior consultant may have to compromise here. Lodging rates for you will vary, depending on which option you choose.

This is when the location of your assignments is most crucial, because it hits your bottom line. For example, if all contract descriptions are created equal, and I'm offered an assignment in NYC or San Francisco versus one paying the same hourly rate in Atlanta, I would choose Atlanta, hands down. Why? Because NYC and San Francisco are two of the most expensive places for temporary relocation.

The bottom line to getting what you want here is based on universal law: Know exactly what you want!

And do your homework. Go to the GSA.gov site and see what the cost of living is for that area when lodging is not covered by the client before you negotiate your rate.

7
YOUR RÉSUMÉ

So, you have a killer résumé. Welcome to the club. You and thousands of other qualified candidates have excellent skills.

The people reviewing your résumé are most likely overwhelmed with work in addition to the stack of other résumés that have now flooded their inbox.

Regardless of your industry, organizing your amazing skills so that they jump out at the reviewer at the client site is the key to landing that first phone screen. Then it's up to you to sell yourself within the first few minutes speaking with the client representative. Long gone are the days when people mailed in their résumés, so different colored paper, or in the 80s scented résumés are a thing of the past. For those of you still hanging on to that mindset, I only have 1 thing to say: *"Hey baby, it's the electronic age. Let's reduce your carbon footprint and save a tree, so, put away that toner cartridge!"*

For project consulting, clients are most interested in the line of business you worked in, the methodologies you know and the technical tools that you've worked with. I begin all the résumés I've submitted with these three sections with column and bulleted information:

- Industries
- Methodologies
- Technical Tools

This immediately grabs the attention of the reviewer, seeing that I have the skill that they're seeking in a candidate, without them having to dig deep within the bullets of the descriptions of my previous assignments to find them.

Of course, I also include this same information within the bulleted description of my assignments, so they can see when I last used the skillset they are seeking.

Other tips include:

- Using present tense verbs to describe your accomplishments, like initiate, perform, build, create, etc.
- Ensure that the tense is the same throughout the résumé.

Don'ts

- Unless you're right out of college or applying for a fulltime assignment, reviewers don't care about your objective, so leave it out.
- And I never put my home address in my résumé for security reasons.
- If you're looking for your next assignment outside your home state, then leave out your current location entirely. This will make sense when you get to the Job Sites and Optimization section.

Résumé writing is an art form. There are many Internet articles to assist you in creating the perfect résumé that will land you an interview.

Looking up the bulleted skills that companies are seeking that align to your skills is an easy free way to fashion them into eye catching bullets for your resume.

If you're still feeling as if yours requires a special touch, then use one of the many services for résumé writing. If it is at or under $100, then it is money well spent.

MULTIPLE VERSIONS OF YOUR RÉSUMÉ

I have a couple of skillsets: Project Management/ Technical Delivery as well as Quality Assurance Program Management.

I find it a great practice to have different versions of your résumé created, highlighting one set of your skills over another when you have varied skills, optimizing your market exposure. When reviewers are looking for the skills to match an assignment, putting those skills as the top bullets of each of your job descriptions will allow them to be easily seen.

For my 3 distinct résumés, I have the same skills, just rearranged to highlight one over the other. I upload the one to the job boards, based on what I feel like doing in my next assignment. That gives me more choices and works for continuing to keep all my skills more current.

ABOUT COVER LETTERS

Many articles will tell you to create detailed cover letters. This is of course your chance to highlight your skillset to potential reviewers. I always submit a cover letter with highlights that reflect where my skills are a match to the job description.

Agencies, however, today often dismiss the cover letter, since submissions in larger firms are performed via an upload in a vendor system, where your résumé is the only file transferred.

8
JOB SITES AND OPTIMIZATION

There are literally hundreds of job boards out there. Depending on your industry and the kind of employment you're seeking, some are more favored than others.

Monster is probably one of the oldest job sites and everyone's heard of it. I find that is more weighted with fulltime jobs or contract-to-hire employment versus consultancy. I still always have at least one active account on Monster when canvasing for my next assignment. You just never know when a client will see your qualifications and offer to make you a deal.

For me, outside of networked agents, DICE is always my first *go to* for technical consulting assignments. There are also plenty of fulltime techie jobs on this site.

One of the newer ones is JuJu. It's connected to many other job sites, allowing you to search over 10 million jobs from all over the web from this one location. This is good if you're interested in looking to apply for jobs, but I am going to teach you how to have your inbox filled with requests for submission from a plethora of agents around the country without applying for a single assignment.

Here's a list of jobs sites of note:

- BestJobsUSA
- CareerBuilder
- CareerCast
- Computerjobs.com
- DICE
- Employment911
- FindARecruiter
- FreshJobs
- Indeed
- Linked In
- Jobs.LiveCareer
- JobSearchShortcut
- JuJu
- Monster
- Simply Hired
- TopjobsUSA
- Vault.com

I also suggest googling Quint Careers top 50 job sites. This is the most comprehensive list I've ever seen, with good descriptions of what each jobsite provides, aiding you in determining the best site to use, based on your industry.

RESUME UPLOADING

When it comes to the option of creating your profile on a job site, never select the short cut version and complete the full profile if that option is offered. You want to be able to edit the employment history and description. Spending the few minutes to set up your profile(s) ahead of time will yield you better results in the long run.

SKILLS KEYWORD OPTIMIZATION

Most job sites will offer you the option of entering your skills, as well as your rating of your expertise of these skills and last used dates. Agents and potential clients looking for talent will search for specific keywords, and job search engines use your skills as part of keyword search returns. Add absolutely every skill you have to these sections.

Multiplying Your Chances of Success

Same Job Site: Same Résumé, Different Locations

I named this optimization *multiplicity,* after the movie where that famous actor Michael K created many versions of himself. In this case, though, you're creating exact duplicate instances of yourself on the same job site, each using a different email address and a different location as your current city.

I may do this for example, if I'm interested in working in either Florida, Arizona or Texas in the winter. I may seek a 4 to 6 month assignment in these locations so I can be out of there before the weather gets disgustingly hot. So, I set up 3 accounts, one for each location on the same job site, each with its own distinct email address. This better ensures that agents looking to fill in these areas easily find me.

When agents contact me, I tell them that I'm seeking to relocate to the area where the contract is located and will do so once I procure my next assignment.

This affords me the opportunity to get paid while I enjoy evenings and weekends in glorious weather. If I play my cards right, I can also get the client to pay for my expenses. Again, a win-win for all, especially me!

Different Job Site: Same Résumé, Different Locations

I named this *Optimization on Steroids,* because of the sheer magnitude of exposure. This is where your résumé presence on the sites goes exponential.

Example: I have my 3 distinct résumés for each 3 desired locations. That's 9 instances of me in total.

Since I have a technique that takes only a couple of minutes to search for a new assignment, having 9 email accounts is not difficult to maintain.

HOW TO RISE TO THE TOP OF JOB SEARCH ENGINES IN LESS THAN 10 MINUTES PER DAY

Want to have your inbox filled with tons of emails from agents begging to submit you to different clients for assignments? This is one of my most favorite tricks, discovering it back in 2003. I received a call from a recruiter who performed a countrywide search for talent. This is when I had 7 accounts targeting 7 locations on one of the job sites. He mentioned that my name came up as the first 7 results in his search. It was then that I realized how the database was structured. From that point, it was a piece of cake.

For this reason, I NEVER APPLY FOR JOBS posted on the job site. That takes too much of my valuable time. I just let the jobs come to me!

You see a job search engine is just a series of relational database tables. Most of these tables are indexed based on DateLastUpdated.

Let me give you an example that will drive this concept home. Have you ever noticed that when you first submit your résumé to a job site, that the first few days you get tons of inquiries about your qualifications? Suddenly, they start tapering off, then after a couple of weeks, you hardly hear a word. Why? Did you suddenly become less marketable? The answer here is no.

What happens is that recruiters usually only reach out the first page of candidates returned from the job search engines that meet the search criteria they entered. Ask yourself how often do you scroll and look at 10 pages deep when you search for something on Google. Ah, I can see the lightbulb illuminating from here.

The trick is to ensure that you're always on the first page. Yes, keywords are vital, but what you want to do is appear to the search engines like you are a new candidate. In tech speak, you want to make sure that your DateLastUpdated is equal to today's date.

I happen to be a little more thorough than that, so depending on which area of the country that I'm canvasing for my next assignment, I will take steps to update some small piece of information in my account *profile* at 9 AM in the prime location where I wish to work every weekday. Even adding and subtracting something simple like a period or comma will do the trick. The systems in these job site engines cannot distinguish the difference of a big change or a small one, so as far as they are concerned you updated your current information. Your DateLastUpdated field now includes the DTS (DateTimeStamp) of the current date and time.

When a recruiter is looking for available candidates that have a specific skill that matches yours, the names returned will be indexed (sorted) on the first page by those that are most recently updated. So, update some small piece of information in your profile each weekday morning and you'll always appear on page 1. It takes 30 seconds to log in and update each job profile you have on these systems to accomplish. By the time your morning coffee is brewed, you'll be done.

HEAVIEST JOB INQUIRY DAYS OF THE WEEK

This is just common sense, but I will state it here so everyone is in the know. Friday afternoons, the weekends, and Monday mornings, are the times when we're getting ready for the weekend, enjoying the weekend or recuperating from it. So, have a beer or Starbucks and toast me, as you enjoy yourself, not expecting many inquiries on the qualifications you posted on job sites. Your best times for expecting the most inquiries are Monday afternoons through Thursday afternoons as you follow the optimization rules I've outlined in this chapter.

APPLYING TO POSITIONS ON THE JOB SITES

So, you found an assignment that seems ideal for you and want to apply. That's great. But know that you will be one of hundreds of résumés the agent or recruiter will receive. If the site lists the name of the recruiter, chances are if you Google their name you may find their direct email address. Place the body of the job title and description into the email along with your cover letter and email it to the contact directly. You will have more of a chance of getting it read if you follow this process.

Before submission do a little more homework.

Perform a search on the title of the position to see if any other agents already have that job posted on the same job site. I would also go a step further and Google that exact job position title to see if it's listed on another job board. If you find duplicates, I would take a close look at the listing and make sure they are the same. Then see if they both list a rate. If they do, chances are one will be greater than another because some agencies are either piggy backing off other agencies or they take a greater percentage of the pay rate that clients are paying.

A Few Words about LinkedIn

No longer is it necessary for you to join a local organization to network.

In recent years, **LinkedIn** has truly become the world's largest Professional **Network**. I held off joining, but when I realized how it's grown, I must tell you that it's really a no-brainer. This venue can be gold for up and rising consultants, so join!

Your Profile

The time you take to put up a profile is invaluable. Take time to add in the companies you worked for using the organization searches. The first thing that agents and company recruiters will see is that familiar company logo next under your work experience area. Because I have several versions of my resume, I make the job title as senior consultant and leave off the detail.

Contacts

Search the site and find the people that you worked with at past jobs. Connect with them and ask them for a recommendation. Getting a couple of recommendations on prior assignments can be the tilt in the scales that lands you that call for an assignment, then subsequent interview, showing recruiters, agents and clients, what others think of your skills.

Agents

Once you put up your profile, you'll have more agents in your home location asking to be one of your new contacts then you know what to do with.

Looking for your next assignment in a different location? The trick is to utilize LinkedIn's keyword search tool, find tuning your search by entering in the zip code within a 100-mile radius of the area you wish to target for your next assignment. Perform this technique for each area you're interested in, and connect with these professionals. After they accept your invitation, write them a quick note telling them that you are relocating to their area once you have procured your next assignment. This will spur them to look at your credentials, tell you if they're the best agent based on your skillset, and may even land you a few solicitations for future assignments in your dream location.

More than 1 LinkedIn Account

You don't have to limit yourself to just 1 account on LinkedIn if there's a vast difference in your experience. I happen to have 2 LinkedIn profiles, one for my technical consultancy and another for my authorship and lecturing. I recommend doing this for individuals who have more than 1 distinct line of business.

WHEN RECRUITERS COME KNOCKING

You probably can imagine the potential hundreds of emails that will flood your inbox when you perform the job optimization tips I have listed above. This also goes for phone calls, so my suggestion is to either remove your phone number from your resume and your profile or put your phone on mute.

Know that there will be good leads and not so good ones, so don't get upset if you are contacted for a software developer job when you are not a developer, because you have a specific keyword in your resume that aligns to software projects. Sometimes to get the Good, you must take the Bad and the Ugly.

Remember, it's when you get no emails that you have a right to be upset.

Just hit the delete button, or you can take a more positive approach like I do, and reply with the following canned response:

Thank you so much for thinking of me, but the job description is not a match to my skillset.

I'm a senior project manager for software development projects, so thanks for updating your system to present me with these types of jobs in future.

If you reply like I do, there is a chance that the person on the other end of the email has a future cherry assignment that would be perfect for you.

9

INTERVIEWING

PHONE, SKYPE OR IN-PERSON

For fulltime positions, there is little chance that you'll not be asked to perform an in-person interview. That makes sense, since the company is going to invest quite a bit of money in you. Typically, you can expect an interested firm to fly you in and reimburse all the expenses you've incurred relative to this interview process.

In consultancy, however, if you're asked to come to the client site, 90% of the time, it's on your dime. If your current location is the same as the location where you're seeking the assignment, it's not a huge time and monetary inconvenience to take a few hours for an in-person interview. Where this can get costly, is if you're seeking an assignment in another state.

With the dawn of the technical age, it's no longer necessary to sit in a room across from interviewers. This is especially true when it comes to consulting. With all the teleconferencing software out there, like Skype, WebEx, BlueJeans, GoTo Meeting, etc., the client still gets the interaction received as if the candidate were sitting right in front of them.

As a matter of practice, I turn down potential assignments where the company is not willing to utilize advances in technology. It just proves to me that they aren't embracing the new way of approaching the interview process and perhaps not keeping up with the times. And if they're not utilizing the newest methodologies and technology, that may be a red flag for being a firm that I want to work with.

EFFECTIVE INTERVIEWING

As I mentioned earlier in this book, always do your homework before your meeting with a potential client. This includes research about the company, their subsidiaries, recent news articles, comments on social media sites and whatever else pops up on Google searches. This is the time to go 10 pages deep and see what you can find out. You can be sure that the people interviewing you are prepared, so you should be too.

For all types of interviews, I make it a practice the day before the interview to devote time to reviewing and comparing my resume to the job description so I am quick to answer questions relating to how my skills will benefit the firm. Some standard questions I have asked or been asked on interviews include detailing how I handled a project that went right, and how I handled a project that went wrong. Traditional questions asked are related to telling interviewers your strengths and weaknesses or areas where you or others think you need improvement.

There are tons of sites on the web that gather standard questions to consider. Again, one of my favorite sources is Quint Careers, whose interview questions database is extensive. The key here is being prepared and not caught off guard. Remember, you won't get a second chance to make a first impression.

A few other practices I follow include:
- Ensuring that I've had something small to eat prior to the interview. Eating nothing or too much can cause you discomfort and become a distraction.

- Smile and sit up straight, even if you are on the phone. This may sound strange, but it does make a difference, whether you are face-to-face with your interviewer or not.
- For in-person or Skype interviews, dress accordingly and keep your legs together with hands in your lap. Direct eye contact is good, but don't stare down your interviewer.
- Answer questions succinctly and briefly with just enough detail without rambling.

The first thing a good interviewer will do is share with your information about the assignment and what they're seeking this consultant to accomplish. Understanding the requirement and the company is key to a successful assignment that benefits all parties, so jot down any questions for later clarification.

After you share all your successes and a couple of failures, there's usually a few minutes for you to ask questions. This is the time when you can ask the client for clarification and the outstanding inquiries you have, to help you determine if this is the right assignment for you, like the methods and technologies being used, if that's your field.

I believe that the end of the interview should also include a couple of sentences thanking the interviewer for their time, as well as stating that you are interested in hearing about next steps, if you want to continue to pursue this assignment.

As soon as the interview is over, call or email the agency and provide them with your thoughts. You can be sure that they will be reaching out to the client for feedback. On a more recent assignment, I texted the agent right after the interview, telling him that the interview went well, and that I wouldn't be surprised if he received an offer that day. The offer came within the hour.

10

WORKING DIRECTLY WITH CLIENTS OR USING AGENCIES

Throughout this book I use terms like agent agencies and recruiters. Most consulting assignments today come through recruiting agencies

In my consultancy, I've had opportunities where clients called me directly to work with them to achieve their business goals through a technical solution. This has always occurred after I have already worked for them in the past on a prior assignment. It's always nice when you receive a direct call from a client asking what it will take for you to come work for them.

More corporations that reach out to you directly will most likely ask you to use one of their designated agencies for legal reasons. This is a formality, since you've already procured the assignment and negotiated the rate, terms and duration.

In the world of consultancy, agencies usually play the role of presenting the requirements for the assignment, handling the interview process, ensuring that you complete all necessary paperwork for onboarding and background compliance and performing on-going payroll processing. In turn, the agency receives a cut on top of the amount promised to you as the consultant. These agents act as your spokesperson for the clients they work with. Because of this, some agencies view themselves as consulting firms, but true consultants view them as the middlemen and administrators that they really are.

Remember, you as the consultant are the talent. Without your expertise, their profits are a big fat zero. There are thousands of agencies all vying for you to become part of their stable. And know that not all agents are created equal. Some large corporations have a handful of main agencies that they use, and smaller agencies work as sub agents for these main agents. This is what I call piggy-backing, where the pay rate the client pays to the main agency is now shared not only with you, but the smaller agency. This ultimately cuts into the rate that you receive as the consultant.

Once you optimize yourself on the job boards and start getting requests for the same assignment from several agencies, you'll start noticing that the descriptions all sound the same, but the rate to the consultant is different.

HOW TO REPLY TO AGENTS FOR OPPORTUNITIES

In the last chapter I talked about your inbox being flooded with more emails than you can open. After selecting the assignments that sound interesting to you, follow this quick checklist to ensure you have the following:

- The Position Title
- Job Description
- The Location
- Type of Employment (Fulltime or Consultancy)
- Assignment Duration
- Rate
- Type of Rate (W2, 1099, Corp-to-Corp)
- Client Name

Chances are if this request comes from an agent, the client's name will be omitted. That's okay for now. Once you establish that the rate is acceptable to you and you provide your resume, the agent will supply you with the name of the client.

Every position will have a title and at a minimum, a high-level description and a location. Some will designate several employment types, the duration as long term and the rate as *market* or *competitive.* That does you little good, since you want specifics.

Below is an example of a canned email that I send to agents that reach out with incomplete information:

Dear Agent:
I looked at the job description that you provided and at first glance it seems that my skills are a perfect match. I'm interested in finding out more. I am accustomed to receiving a minimum per hour W2 rate of $$$.

I appreciate your reply to this email detailing the assignment duration in months, as well as telling me if the rate offered to the consultant meets my minimum standards.

This puts the ball back in their court and forces them to reply to your email, especially if your phone number is not posted. This way you can enjoy your coffee in peace as you get to the next email in the long list you now have.

Some agents will respond with a rate that is so much lower than you would accept, asking you if you would consider it. I never say never and if I'm desperate for an assignment I may have to consider it. Most times, I graciously reply, *"I'm going to pass on this opportunity."*

PRIOR TO SUBMISSION

Over the years I've been contacted by hundreds of agents. As I mentioned they are not created equal. For example, there is a large disparity when it comes to how consultants are paid. Maybe this no longer applies, but I always asked the following questions of the agency prior to using them as my mouthpiece.

What pay schedule do you use for your consultants?

The best agencies will pay their consultants weekly. This puts more money in your pocket per month if you're paid on W2. Bi-weekly is also one of the norms today. When I hear of a consulting firm that is still paying consultants bi-monthly or monthly, I won't use them. This is where you really must be cautious. I've worked with a couple of small and medium sized agencies and was concerned whether I would be paid. There was a more recent contract where I logged into my agency provided email account after my 4th day to find over 200 late payment notices from their existing consultants in my inbox. I immediately reached out to my agency contact stating that I must have been mistakenly added to the internal accounts receivable team distribution list and was receiving emails that I should not be seeing.

Do you have direct deposit?

If an agency in this era does not offer their consultants direct deposit, do not use them. You'll thank me later when you receive each and every paycheck that you are entitled to in a timely fashion.

A FEW VERSUS MANY

Working with a few key agents in different market places is *one* way to optimize your successes. The good thing about agents is that if you don't like one agent, there are literally thousands ready to take their place.

If you're first establishing yourself, or want to optimize your chances of hearing about every available position that could be a match to your skills, then being open to dealing with several agencies as you discover the ones that you like, versus the ones that you don't is not a terrible idea.

Working with several agencies provides you with the advantage of being presented with more available positions in the marketplace.

RIGHT TO REPRESENT

Some agencies will often have you sign a right to represent or an exclusivity agreement prior to submission. This has its advantages as well as drawbacks, so ensure that you never sign a blanket exclusive right to represent you for a specified time period.

There are many positions available for a large client and the only right to represent that I sign these days relates to a specific job with a corresponding position number. This protects me from arguments that may arise from double submissions, but also allows me the freedom of being submitted to several different positions in the same corporation by different vendor agencies.

ASKING FOR REFERENCES UP FRONT

There are a couple of agencies out there that will remain nameless, who will not start the submission process for an opportunity until they speak to your references. I had a few agents from this same company contact me regarding jobs in a few different places across the country. Each one told me the same thing. It didn't matter that one of their associates had already spoken to my references. They had to speak to them personally.

Imagine if every agent requested this, and you'll soon understand why I'm against this policy. It is for this reason that I do not deal with these agencies.

Your references are worth their weight in gold, so respect their time and stay in their favor. Being contacted more than twice a year is an annoyance, especially if they are references to more than one person.

Have your references handy, but hold onto them until the client wants to offer you the assignment. Then your references can sing your praises to the client, and to you afterward, for procuring your next gig.

NEGOTIATING THE BEST DEAL

This is where it can get a little tricky, because the agent and client are trying to get you to accept the lowest rate possible to maximize their profits, while keeping you happy. On the other hand, you want to be able to maximize your own pocketbook.

Remembering that the agency is nothing more than a middleman and payroll administrator, helps put things in perspective. They aren't going to hang up on you if you ask for an increase in the rate after you have had the initial phone screen. Remember, you *are* their bread and butter.

There have been plenty of times that I've come back to an agent after an initial phone screen stating that I liked the position, but that the job is more expansive than the initial description that the agent supplied. It always is, since agents only get a high-level description. This puts you in a good position to leverage this statement you have made when the client makes an offer. When the agent reaches out to you telling you that the client wants you to start right away, this is when you get to use that leverage statement that I reference above and ask for another $5 per hour, *"Well, Mr. Agent, as I mentioned when we spoke after the interview, the assignment is much more expansive than you initially communicated. I cannot see doing it for less than $$$."*

The agent is already counting the money that you'll generate for his company and their first reaction may not be cordial.

Take a deep breath and know that the only thing in life that you have control over is your reaction, so close your mouth and remember this:

The cooler and non-emotional you are, the more money per hour you'll acquire.

Silence is your best weapon. If you get emotional you're only telling the agent that there is really some wiggle room here. Expect to settle for half that amount, $2.5, but remember that every additional dollar you receive equates to $2000 per year, and that extra $2.5 per hour equates to $5000. That can equate to a 3 week all-expense paid trip to China or wherever your vacation will take you after the assignment is over.

Keeping your cool has its advantages.

GETTING TRAVEL AND LODGING EXPENSES PAID

Having the client pay for your expenses is also a great area to negotiate. Usually it's customary to sort this out prior to submission, but there are occasions where I have negotiated expense payments prior to starting. Sometimes, I negotiated partial remote work after the assignment began.

I don't always feel comfortable asking a client to pay for my meals, since I must eat regardless of where I'm located. This is of course up to you as you discussed reimbursed expenses with the agent.

Just remember this: A client will move heaven and earth to get you if they think that you add value.

CONTRACTS

You're required to sign an employment contract with the agency as part of your arrangement. Please read this carefully prior to signing, but note that most if not all agencies will not allow you to alter the agreement in any way. That's why it's very important to negotiate the terms of the agreement prior to accepting the position.

Non-Compete Clause

Also expect to see a non-compete clause in the agreement that you sign with every agency you work with. A non-compete clause states that you will not be allowed to work for the client company for a specified time after the contract ends unless you procure that work through that firm. With that said, I have never seen a penalty if you decide to accept a full-time position with the client company during your consultancy engagement. The typical non-compete timeframe I have seen is 12 months. I will not work with any agency that has a period of greater that a 12-month period.

HIGHER APPROACHES TO CONSULTANCY

I once worked alongside a senior consultant. He did very little in the way of work, but bragged about the great deal he'd negotiated with the client and confided that his intention was to do as little work as possible. Every Friday by early midday he would shut down his computer and leave. I had lunch with him one afternoon, where he shared with me his qualifications. He was very sure of himself, and stated that the only reason that he took the assignment was that it would look good on his résumé.

He boasted about a large initiative that once managed and how it went over by 2 years. I sat there thinking to myself, "Why is this guy bragging about what I would consider a failure?"

To me, getting the client to the goal post on time and within budget is a success. Anything less than that is less than stellar if it within your control. When I questioned him on it, he turned to me and smiled, "Well, I got another 2 years out of them. And my bank account was stuffed."

Sure, we all want to be able to replenish our bank accounts and add skills for our next assignment. In all my years of consulting, I've never spent time at a client with such a non-caring person. I would never just up and leave if I had a deadline, but ask if a task will bring me over a normal work week, if they would like me to complete it with overtime hours.

No matter if I'm doing a small gig or a large one, I truly care about my clients and want only the best work product. Having a do what it takes attitude to get the job done is the mark of a superior consultant.

Rework Rule

I have this rule. If I see that the client is doing something that is going to cause them delays, failure or rework, I feel compelled to bring it up to them to ensure that they are aware of a potential cost savings based on the timeliness of a deliverable.

When I was working an assignment with big pharma, I was asked to create a rather time-consuming deliverable. I knew that we were waiting on many pieces and the chances of having to totally rework it had a 100% probability. I just had to tell the client that of course I can provide them with what they were seeking, but that the entire thing was not going to be useable in about 4 weeks and that it would have re-created, most likely from scratch. They did not seem to care about the rework. I asked them again, if they were sure that it would not be more cost effective to wait and create it only once. After that second ask, I stopped and provided them with what they wanted, knowing that I would be creating it again. No one ever balked at the rework 2 months down the road. As a matter of fact, I was provided with accolades for the rewrite.

Adding Value

The job of a consultant is simple. Jump in and add value. Over the years I've led and driven many projects to success from the pre-Y2K crisis to today.

It's when I've being able to add value and helped the client achieve their goals do I feel successful.

Therc are, however been a couple of assignments over the past 20 years where I've gotten a client to a certain point, but an insurmountable barrier keeps the program from moving forward. This is not your ordinary barrier, for being in project management, I experience those all the time. I'm talking about the big ones, like when the methodology does not have the buy-in from key stakeholders. From where I come from this is a big no-no. But it happens.

So, what is a consultant to do when they are presented with something that is sure to cause a program to fail? Well, the male associate I mention above, loves these situations, because it means he can continue to line his pockets until the program is finally shut down.

Me on the other hand, I have a different philosophy. I will work until I drop to help my current client, but if in my heart I know that if I can no longer add value, then I express my feelings about it and excuse myself.

OTHER ITEMS OF NOTE

Vacation

As a consultant, you are usually not entitled to paid holidays or paid vacation days, unless that is something that you negotiate with the agency you are working with prior to the start of the assignment. It does happen though on occasion that an agency will pay part or all your health benefits as well as provide you with some paid vacation. In my experience, this is the exception and not the rule, but again this is a negotiating point. When it comes to taking vacation, paid or otherwise, if you have a planned vacation in less than 6 months of the start of a contract, please tell this to your agent prior to beginning the assignment in writing. Managing theirs and the client's expectation is a sure-fire way to gain initial respect.

Benefits

Any agency that tells you that they don't have any benefits, especially now with Health Care regulations in force is being less than truthful. They must provide information on health benefits, allowing you to make the choice whether to purchase them or not.

Mandatory Furloughs

Please consider that some firms are now instituting 1 to 2 week periods during the calendar year where consultants are asked to stay home. I have seen this typically occur during the last 2 weeks of the year around the holiday. And what does a consultant do during this period? Right, they take a vacation, spend time with family and enjoy life. It's prudent to perform some due diligence here to find out if this is the case in the firm that you are working with, since this time off is unpaid and plan accordingly.

Miscellaneous

When working on an assignment for a large financial firm, they instituted a policy that after 6 months they reduced the pay rate for the agency by 5%. They reduced it again another 5% after 9 months, then again at 12 months for a total 15% pay rate reduction in the first year. Now this financial firm had a few approved vendors (agencies) that they used who were making millions from the work efforts of the consultants that were brought to this client. Some of these agencies decided that they would pass on the reduction of pay to their consultants. When the policy came into force, they sent an email to all their consultants stating that if they didn't sign it, then they would not be permitted to continue working at the client site. These agencies thinking was flawed. The consultants have already gained valuable experience at the client site. This strong-arm fear based tactics is unethical.

Any idea how that worked out? Right!

A small percentage decided to immediately walk off the job and within the first year that the new policy took force, the consultants started leaving in mass.

Since that time, I was asked by a firm to agree to a reduction prior to submission when being asked to work once more with this client. I refused to sign the agreement stating that if the client was going to reduce the pay rate to the agency, it was not going to be me that would be taking the hit.

That policy has been abandoned the following year.

I point this out because you have a responsibility to try and find out as much as you can about the agencies that you choose to work with.

Doing your homework on the agency as well as the client will alleviate potential headaches down the road.

Become a Consultant

11
HITTING THE GROUND RUNNING

GETTING UP TO SPEED

Consultancy is not like working as a fulltime employee of a firm. As a fulltime employee, it is typical to have 6 months or more to get up to speed as you learn all the ins and outs of the lines of business, process and systems.

In my experience, consultancy on the other hand, leaves you with little assimilation time before you are expected to be productive. But that's what the firm is paying you for. You are the expert, or the hired gun as I have called it. You've been brought in, usually during crisis mode or chaos situations to help quench the fire.

For me, these situations are when I get to show my best skills, as I come up with ideas and processes to help firms move forward once more.

It's not a position for the passive, although I still must learn balance when my more assertive tendencies may lean toward being viewed as aggressive. It's remembering that ideas can be aggressive and progressive, but not allowing them to come across as personal aggression.

One of the first things I do when coming into a firm, is to start by digesting the corporate hierarchy of the teams, creating contact lists of the lines of business and technical teams I am going to be working with.

I ensure that I keep on top of all the system accesses that I need. Being diligent to ensure that all the pieces are in place to do the job is key. Every link I'm provided is bookmarked so I can quickly return to it when needed.

The first few weeks is always a little difficult, having me question why I took the assignment in the first place. After week 3, I feel a little more comfortable and really start contributing. By week 6, I usually come up with some great idea and management notices my worth.

ASSIMILATING INTO THE CULTURE TO GAIN INSIGHT

Knowing how to dress in the workplace can be crucial to success. When I worked in management consulting, it was mandatory to wear basic Brooks Brother's suits, with men darning ties, tab collars and cuff links. I found when working in firms with very casual dress codes, that wearing a suit just makes you stand out and puts off the day-to-day employees that are your bread and butter for information. Some management consulting firms haven't figured that out yet, but I can tell you that there's a delicate balance when you're a consultant. Your main initial goal is to establish relationships and get the information you need to do the job, so you can ultimately help the company be successful.

I'll never forget an assignment I had where I was in a one-horse town. I quickly learned that I better where jeans and a tee shirt to quickly assimilate into the culture. So, I went to the local Walmart and purchased a couple of pairs of cheap jeans and tee shirts. By my second week I started receiving lunch invitations from the local staff.

On another assignment with a bunch of young techies, there was a foosball table in the break room. I brushed off a skillset that I hadn't used in decades and asked to join in. When they realized that I had an awesome kill shot I was welcomed with open arms.

It was at these lunches and over foosball matches where they spilled all the secrets, like defects with current processes and grievances about being short staffed in their area. This information is priceless on an assignment and can take months of analysis to uncover. I utilized it to assist in improvement suggestions. Some call these quick hits, as they are the sparkling gems in a consultant's repository. They make the consultant look good, not only to executive management, but also win favor with the day-to-day work staff. It's a win-win all around.

One of the tips I'll share that I've learned over the years when dealing with company culture, especially organizations where staff is from another country, is to learn a little bit about their native culture as a talking point. Also knowing a few words in several native tongues, like hello, and thank you can immediately break down a potential barrier and make an instant ally.

12
VIEWS OF CONSULTANTS

CORPORATE VIEWS ON CONSULTANTS

Over the past decade, I've seen a shift in the workforce. With increased corporate flexibility, more positions are lending themselves to consultancy. I believe that part of this change has been driven by advances in technology.

The other piece of the puzzle is the way that corporations view their bottom line in their asset valuation for shareholders. They view consultants as temporary and as such the fees paid for these hired experts is expensed differently on the company's general ledger.

CONSULTANT HURDLES

Often when a consultant is engaged to work with existing long-term staff, there may be a few hurdles that they need to jump over.

Existing company employees may view a consultant's presence as a threat to their job security, when an expert, who most likely comes into a firm with superior skills, can quickly assess the situation, and make suggestions on process improvement. Let's face it. If things were running smoothly and on target, within defined deadlines and budget, there'd be little need for us to be there, but for most consultants, taking an assignment to get someone else's job cannot be farther from the truth. In my consultancy, I want to get in there, do the job, and then cheerfully leave when the assignment is over. I've never had designs on becoming a fulltime employee at the expense of someone else.

Some hurdles can feel more like barriers to success. I remember working with the staff of a company where the women who needed to provide me with information where not pleased that I was there. I sat right next to one of them usually listening to music. In this instance, the music had stopped, but I didn't remove my headphones.

What I heard was this gal speaking on the phone stating the following, *"I am holding back the systems password from the consultant to make them look bad."*

After she hung up the phone, I peeked my head around the cubicle, asking to speak to her privately. In that conversation, I explained that I was only there to do the assignment, then leave. The sooner she supplied me with what I needed, the faster I would be out the door. I also added, what today I would term as a more flippant comment, which was, *"Just because my headphones are on, doesn't mean the music is playing."*

HAVING A TOUGH SKIN

You must have a tough skin if you're going to be a consultant. This is at times easier said than done when dealing with existing staff. I have had instances like the one mentioned above where existing employees have stooped to sabotage. It's not always easy to take these instances in stride, but as a consultant, you can't take anything personally.

In other writing, I talk about knowing that the only thing we have control over is our reaction.

I can say that if I were perfect, then I would probably be retired now on some tropical island. I try my best to catch myself before reacting to the fear-based behavior of existing staff, that feel threatened by the presence of an expert in their midst.

Consulting was once deemed as a men's club and for a time it was more challenging for women. Although it is getting better, there are still some men that don't like to be told that what they are currently doing needs improvement, especially when it is coming from a woman. Certain cultures also still view women today as an inferior sex, so to the women who want to break into this arena, you need to know that coming in.

I have a friend who was working as a consultant in a health organization. She never was made to feel welcome in the 1.5 years of the assignment, where the typical full-timer she worked with had 30 years tenure. We talked about this and she smiled after she realized that she was making double the amount of those woman on the job site.

Things are getting better, because not many stay in an organization for their entire career anymore, which lends itself to less office politics and pettiness. If you're looking for a family in an organization as a consultant, then you're not in the right field.

13
ONSITE LODGING OPTIONS

There are many lodging options when you are onsite in an out-of-state location. These include:

- Temporary Corporate Apartments
- Motels and Hotels
- Private Roommate Rentals
- Apartment or small house
- The Traveling Nomad

TEMPORARY CORPORATE APARTMENTS

These are fully furnished turnkey 1 and 2 bedroom apartments located in an existing apartment complex. They include all cable, internet, electric, furnishings, linens, towels and kitchenware. They usually rent monthly and are typically 2-3 times higher than the apartment's normal rent. This is one of the easiest options, albeit the most expensive. Just bring your suitcase and once unpacked, you're ready to hit the ground running.

MOTELS AND HOTELS

There is certainly a lot of variety when it comes to motels and hotels. Most hotels offer daily rates, with some motels offering weekly rates. Choosing one of these options may get you a small refrigerator and microwave, perhaps a modest breakfast, but nothing more.

If I choose this option I price out the hotel for 1 week in each month for the expected contract duration, to better determine if I'm going to get slammed by their seasonal rates at a certain time of the year.

Since tastes vary widely, I will leave it up to you in determining if the Motel 6 is part of the places you would consider

There may be a couple of long stay hotel options available where you are consulting, that will include a scaled down kitchen. This is one of the options I choose most often when I know I am not going to be in a place for a year or more.

PRIVATE ROOMMATE RENTALS

When I was a bit younger, this was a viable option for me. Some people will advertise monthly rooms for rent on craigslist. Ads will tell you whether the room is furnished or unfurnished.

APARTMENT OR SMALL HOUSE?

If you know that you're going to be onsite for 9 months or more, you may consider renting an apartment or small house. If you get a furnished residence, then you don't have to concern yourself with purchasing all the things you need to get set up.

Setup costs can get pricey, but there are a couple of alternatives here. You can rent an entire apartments worth of furniture and housewares from places like Cort furniture rental.

You can also be a bit more adventurous. For example, if you rented a studio that has a breakfast bar, you could get away with 2 stools and a hammock with a stand. Having spent so much time in Mexico and South America over the past decades, I'm just as comfortable in a hammock that any bed I've ever slept in. Again, it all comes down to taste and lifestyle.

THE TRAVELING NOMAD

In this time of tiny houses, more people are living the nomad lifestyle. I know several consultants that cart their tiny house or traveling trailer/RV to the general area where they are working and find monthly or free places to set up their temporary homestead during their assignment.

In addition to RV parks, this includes free camping sites in nearby state parks. You do not feel like you're missing anything with a cell phone with an internet hotspot and a large roof mounted solar panel.

Kate is a consultant who works remotely as a graphic designer. She has no home base, but works from the mini-bus she converted to a tiny house as she migrates from one national park to another.

14

Accounting and Taxes

Accounting and Essential Tools

Having good organizational skills as a consultant is crucial to your success when it comes to accounting.

There's a few musts here that I must share:

- Get an Accountant

- Save all your receipts

- Create spreadsheets to organize and categorize expenses

Accountant
I really don't care if your cousin Billy has been doing your taxes for the past 20 years or you have been using one of those firms that set up shop with seasonal workers in the local Walmart at tax time.

Hiring an accountant may cost you a little more money per year, but they are well versed with the newest tax codes and will provide you with sound advice and best way to account for the tax right offs for your consultancy.

Receipts

It's important to save and organize all your receipts, regardless of whether the company is reimbursing your expenses or you're paying them yourself. This is especially true when you're traveling every week as receipts add up quickly and you may have a few dozen by each week's end.

I tally them weekly when traveling, then place each week's receipts into a labeled envelope in case I need to go back to them for accounting or at a client's request. Some of the people I have worked with also scan them, since over a few years the ink on receipts fades.

Spreadsheets

One of the essential tools of a consultant is a few specially crafted spreadsheets and folders set up on your computer.

I create a master spreadsheet with 12 tabs, each representing a month of the year along with auto-calculating summary tab. I enter the amount from each receipt into a category in a spreadsheet that is totaled by type for that month. This makes it easier for me at tax time to print the summary tab to send the category totals to my accountant for the most accuracy.

You will find this year's spreadsheet under the Tools menu on LDForester.com

Paycheck City

If you're 100% onsite at a location in a different state, the agency will withhold state tax based on the location where you're working. Free online tools like Paycheck City will help you calculate the state tax that will be withheld from your paycheck. You may be able to argue this with the agency if you work remote part of the week or month from your home state, so taxes withheld are based on your home state.

A note to remember though is about W2 consulting. When the assignment ends, unless you were fired with cause, you are most likely entitled to receive unemployment as you canvas for your next gig. That almost sounds like a paid vacation, doesn't it?

This depends on your base period. For those of you who don't know this, the unemployment eligibility base period is usually the first four of the last five completed calendar quarters prior to the time that you file your unemployment claim.

So, what does that mean to you?

Well, let's say that you live in Florida, but worked in Boston for 3 months during the base year prior to the end of the assignment and your agency took out Massachusetts taxes for that timeframe.

That means that instead of collecting unemployment from Florida and getting $275 a week, you can file with Massachusetts at $742 a week.

I was advised that it only takes 1 paycheck with taxes withheld in a state during the base period to qualify for unemployment benefits for that state, but please do your own research on eligibility. You can also google, *Maximum Weekly Unemployment Benefits by State* to see the benefits by each state.

W2 VERSUS 1099 VERSUS CORP-TO-CORP

There are 3 income types that consultants can receive:

- W2
- 1099
- Corp-to-Corp

W2

W2 consultancy is not much different taxwise than working for a company, considering that you receive a paycheck each pay period and the number of hours you work each week. Depending on your assignment and agreement overtime hours are permitted, logged and paid. The agency pays the employer tax portion based on your rate.

When working through an agency I opt for W2 employment when expenses are reimbursed.

As of the 2017 tax code, unreimbursed expenses are recorded as part of itemized deductions (Sch A).

With the changes in the 2018 tax code based on recent legislation that President Trump has passed, it may be more beneficial to always have the client reimburse expenses if you are W2 worker or opt for 1099 or Corp-to-Corp and write them off on their respective tax forms, especially if your write-offs do not exceed the standard Schedule A deductions for short term engagements. Lease seek the advice of your accountant for what works best in your situation.

Remember, you can negotiate something with the agent that would perhaps allow you up to a$3000 a month cap on reimbursed expenses so you can forgo itemization for these expenses.

Remember, everything in consulting is negotiable!

1099
When you agree to a 1099 assignment, you get the rate times the hours work with no taxes withheld. You will receive a form 1099 at year end and you are responsible for both the employer and employee portion of Federal and State taxes.

This may be a better option when you're working with unreimbursed expenses as you will record these deductions on a form other than the one used to itemize your personal deductions. Again, please seek the advice of an accountant for your specific situation.

I have worked 1099 and the invoicing and payments are usually monthly.

Corp-to-Corp

Corp to Corp (C2C) means that the client corporation or agency pays your corporation for services rendered.

Typically, C2C's invoice a client Bi-monthly. Your accountant will be able to advise you on the avenue that works best for your situation.

15
MAXIMIZING PERKS

There are perks gained when consulting, some of which I have already hinted at in this book.

Hotels
When I travel for assignments and stay at local hotels, regardless whether the client or I am picking up expenses, I always ensure that I stay at hotels where I have signed up for loyalty membership. Most hotels have special point offerings as well during certain times of the year and points earned during assignments add up quickly. I also have cards that are associated with hotel chains, so I am getting extra incentive points when I use my card to pay my hotel bill.

Airlines
Airlines also reward their loyalty members as do rental car companies and local eating establishments.

I also get rewards by using certain credit cards to book my flights and they usually provide enough miles when you join and spend a minimum amount for a free airline ticket. Using the same airline for weekly travel will get you to an elite status in no time and give you automatic upgrades and other incentives.

Rental Cars

Rental car companies reward their loyalty members. I have memberships in 3 and no longer have to wait at the counter, but have my name posted on the board and go straight to my car. I keep an eye out on their websites on their monthly incentives allowing me to choose the rental car firm for that trip that provides me the best points.

Food

There are several food chains that offer perks for frequent diners. Even Starbucks has a loyalty program, so drink up and enjoy, especially when you are being reimbursed for food.

Summary

It may not seem like it, but things really add up to become big perks, even on a 6-month gig.

After a 6-month partial week travel assignment ends, I book my month-long vacation with free airfare, I stay at hotels free of charge, depending on my hotel status and chain, I get a free cooked to order breakfast each day of my stay, enjoy a free rental car and at least a couple of free good meals and free morning coffee.

16
WHAT TO DO WHEN THE
ASSIGNMENT ENDS

So, your assignment is about to end. This is where the consultant differs from the fulltime employee. When a fulltime employee finds out that they're going to be laid off, they get very upset, sometimes, depressed, or panicked. This is because they define themselves by their job and title and most likely live at or above their means.

Consultants on the other hand, get excited when they know that their last day is coming. That's because it's time for vacation. Clients are usually pretty good about telling their consultants a few weeks ahead of time when the assignment is ending. This has always been my signal to book an airline ticket to some exotic place I have not yet visited.

While full-timers are crying into their pillows, the consultant that has planned well for the time in between assignments starts acting like a child knowing that they are going to visit Disneyland.

TIME OFF SAVINGS

If you'd like to enjoy your time off in between assignments there a couple of things that you'll need to plan for. Savings is one of them.

Ideally, you want to have money in your account to cover your bills for 6-8 months. That may sound like a lot of Moola to some of you, but if you want to take 6 months off and travel to Machu Picchu, you want to do it without worrying that you'll have to cut your trip short.

17

HOW TO LIVE AS A CONSULTANT

I wanted to take this time to discuss how consultant's live. Unlike most people I have a very small footprint. Don't get me wrong, I live very comfortably, enjoying lavish pampering, massages and spa weekends as well as dining in fine restaurants. What I mean is that I don't accumulate a lot of material possessions. I don't collect gadgets or oversized items. I do however collect experiences as I move from assignments in between periods when I am *on vacation.*

Most consultants have a home base. Of course, for me the best assignments are remote in nature, but if traveling for a gig, perhaps your home base is located in a state that has no state tax, a home in an area that's not subject to weather extremes or a place that can easily be locked up and left without the worry of freezing pipes over the winter. Better yet, maybe you have a home base in a location that becomes a vacation rental when you are on assignment. That's always a nice extra bang for your buck.

When you must be at the client site during the work week, you have to make a choice to either rent out or lock up your home-based residence and move 100% of the time to the onsite location, or travel onsite during the week and travel back home on the weekends.

There's also a third option, and that's having a home base that's nothing more than a PO Box and a storage unit. There was a woman named Michele who I met while on assignment in New York City who did just that. Her company paid for her travel and onsite expenses. Each weekend, she would fly to a different city where friends and family lived keeping her expenses to a minimum while taking an advantage of continued mini vacations.

Whichever option you choose, know that it's important to ensure that it's cost effective for your situation and know the tax benefits and consequences of the choice you're making.

About Enough

In an earlier chapter I mentioned about that incredible Porsche 911, that I had enough money to buy in cash after an assignment. I strolled into the dealership knowing exactly what I wanted. I white knuckled the salesman during my test drive, as I hugged the curves of the road at the perfect angle and accelerated, just shy of losing control. When we returned, I told him that I was going to go to lunch and would contact him later that day.

As I sat in a local diner, I contemplated the purchase. I worked my butt off non-stop for 2 years and I was ready for my reward. From the couple of cars that I had purchased in the past, my process was to do my research, know what I wanted before walking into the dealership, test drive the car, then negotiate a price and drive it off the lot. For some reason though, today would be different.

Then it hit me like a ton of bricks.

I knew that if I bought this car, I would be ecstatic for a week or two, but I really didn't need that car.

It was that day that I figured out what enough was.

I didn't buy that car, but decided instead to take a 3-month journey backpacking through parts of Peru in South America, following the life of ancient tribes that inhabited the area. That cost me about $4000 and left my bank account full of cash.

Not too long after I returned from Peru, was the 9/11 attack on the World Trade Center. It was a time of great grieving for the country. It was also a time when all consulting assignments were put on hold or cancelled. In hindsight, I am glad that I didn't buy that Porsche.

The point of this story is that with consulting the only guarantee you have is... well wait, there *are* none.

I drive this point home, because there are no guarantees of continued paychecks, no golden parachutes and no severance packages.

Taking what you earn and saving a good portion of it is the only way you can afford to live like a beach bum in Bali for 6 months before canvassing for your next consulting assignment.

Living smaller than your means and having at least 6 months in savings in addition to money for fun vacations is the way of the successful consultant.

Don't assume that the money you've amassed will continue indefinitely. Don't feel like you must keep up with your neighbors, those poor schmucks who live from paycheck to paycheck supersizing everything they purchase from top designer clothes to the bed sheets to their underwear. Objects are part of the prestigious badge that most use to define success and it is not the best and newest technological gadgets, televisions, and upgraded computers that will sustain your consultant lifestyle.

Remember, just because you can afford 3 cars does not mean that you should own 3 cars.

Living in lack is something a consultant never do. We do not live beyond their means, where consultants live below, saving dollars for the times *we choose* not to work and travel. We do not live paycheck to paycheck.

If the answer is that something is lacking in your life, then you have just taken a step toward realizing a possible solution and more avenues toward happiness.

Fear and Risk

Fear will always keep you from realizing your true potential.

My dad was a truly amazing man, with a degree like mine focused in mathematics. He worked for several firms early in his career, then leveraged his assets to follow his passion of being self-employed. He had several businesses and partnerships including percentages in New York City based restaurants, construction companies, and entertainment venues. He also was heavily involved in real estate, buying and renting many of the small homes in the surrounding towns a few miles away from my Long Island childhood residence. He created a positive cash flow that afforded us a comfortable lifestyle. Although my dad was not a traditional consultant, he was not afraid to try something new or take risks. It was that lack of fear that helped drive him forward and was the foundation that he left me with.

I'll never forget when I was about 7 years old when he started me working as a paid consultant for him, doing payroll. I counted the money and verified it against the amount shown on the outside of the envelope stuffed and sealed it. I was paid $2 a week for my time. That may not seem like a lot of money to kids today but it was a fortune to me at that time.

Self-Worth and Self Esteem

Self-esteem is our belief *about* ourselves, while self-worth is the value we place *on* ourselves.

Self-worth and self-esteem are closely tied together and are probably the 2 most *underrated* core beliefs that we face as humans. Why underrated? Because when we master them, we become so powerful the possibilities are endless. It's when we value ourselves and know that we *add* value to every situation, that we have achieved a healthy balance of self-esteem and self-worth.

This is so important when speaking about consultancy. Why? Because you must believe in yourself and your value to best serve the needs of the client and organization.

It is this confidence and value of self that spurs you to speak up when you see something broken in an organization, without the fear that you'll lose favor or the assignment.

Having a dad like mine, who built up my self-esteem, it's no wonder why I think outside-the-box, have an entrepreneurial spirit and take risks as I venture into uncharted territories in all parts of my life.

This is the kind of spirit that consultants need to have. If you combine lack of fear and calculated risk taking, with good organizational skills, you'll be a star for sure.

www.ingramcontent.com/pod-product-compliance
Lightning Source LLC
Chambersburg PA
CBHW071005040426
42443CB00007B/670